Me.

He█ █,

GOD

What Her Depression Taught Me

MELISSA SAMUELS

Manufactured in the United States of America
10 9 8 7 6 5 4 3 2 1
Library of Congress Cataloging-in-Publication Data is available.

ISBN: 978-1-68556-695-1
E-ISBN: 978-1-68556-696-8

*What many don't know
about depression
and what doctors will not tell you.*

Dedication

To my awesome daughter, Kiki.

You have made such an impact on my life. I see how God used you to break and rebuild me. You are my inspiration. Love, Mom.

For all the mothers and girls going through, you are not alone.

Acknowledgments

To the kingdom of love.

To my friend and now pastor, Pastor Smith, I love this man of God and thank God for him. Without his guidance and wisdom, I would not be where I am today. You have been such a tower of strength and constant help to my family. May God bless you continually. Much love, M.O.G.

To Pastor Cross, whose little words of wisdom and nuggets shared in brief chats and reflection helped me. Thank you for helping me to see things clearer. I remember when the light bulb came on after you said something in a meeting. Much love, M.O.G.

To Chanel, my sister. You have been a help to me, a friend, and a listening ear. Love you, sis. Thank you. May God enlarge your borders.

To Nicolette. Wow, sis, wow. The little viper I call you. Thank you for your prayers, my sister, much love.

To the famous couple, the Shepherds, may God continue to bless and keep you both. Much love and thanks for your prayers.

To sis Niki. Girl, you rock. Thank you for the prayers and encouragement. Much love.

To Suzi Q, the top topper. Your kindness and humble character encourage me. Thank you for your prayers.

Appreciation

Throughout the whole ordeal, I was blessed to have the help of the middle school's social worker, who stood by us and would come to the apartment to ensure that my child was getting ready for school. God bless this wonderful woman. (Her name is withheld intentionally.) I also had a great sister, Rochel, who is so dear to me. I love this girl as my own blood. She prayed with me, visited my child at the hospital when I couldn't, and was with me in the ups and downs. I had, too, the prayers and care of our Bible college study group, Thirteen. Then there were the Wrights, who took my daughter in a few weekends and cared for her. This gave me time to rest and do needed assignments. May God bless and keep you always. Thank you all for your generosity to my girl and for trying.

To my sister, who tried, I do appreciate the times you spoke to her and had her over. Thank you. God knows I love you. To my dad, thank you for being a source for her and someone she can turn to. I appreciate you all who were there in the beginning of the journey. Thank you.

To her therapist, who always had our back, Ms. P, thank you. To the doctor, I appreciate you and your knowledge. To Kiki's grandmothers and to everyone who touched our lives in some way or the other, may God bless you.

Table of Contents

Introduction

I thank my God, who saw fit to allow me this experience so that I can bless others and, with the help of the Holy Spirit, open their eyes to the unseen realm around us. We know that mental illness is real and that these things are influenced by spirits in the unseen realm. The Word says that we wrestle against principalities and powers, *not* men.

Before I had this experience, I was in church at a youth meeting. The topic of depression came up as someone was sharing about a person in their class who was cutting themselves. Then another youth shared a similar experience as they too had a friend who had depression. My response was, "This is a spirit; how can a young child be experiencing depression?" One adult replied and said that it was not a spirit and that children are really depressed. Another said that it was both. Today I still hold to my belief. Depression is influenced by evil spirits with the sole intention of destroying the individual, young or old. Once the individual is destroyed, there goes their dreams, potential, and possible lifting of the family and or nation. A year after that discussion in the back of the church, my own daughter was diagnosed with depression.

God allowed me my very own experience, and I'm sharing it with those who were and are skeptical. Today my daughter is not where she was. No medication helped her. We tried it. Therapy only cooled a hot situation for a while, but the true results began to manifest after consistent prayer and changes in my own lifestyle/mindset, how I responded and dealt with each pressing day.

Let the thing you'll hear and learn bless you. Let it show you another way, the only way to lasting results and peace. Have an open mind, and don't knock it until you try it. I know what I'm saying; I've lived it. Upon writing this book, the deliverance hadn't come to fruition, only in small pieces. I asked, "Lord, how can I write when there are still things that need to be corrected in my child?" But the Holy Spirit encouraged me to write and not to worry about the end; it will come. So, I want to encourage readers to be optimistic as they go through their trials, knowing that Christ is with you always. He will never leave us nor forsake us. He is faithful.

The Beginning

"Lady, weh you man deh (where is your man)?" This was the question Kiki asked the lady in the supermarket. She was only three years old at the time. I was shopping for her weekly grocery. This was our weekly routine together. I walked down the aisle, pushing her in the baby seat of the shopping cart. She was wearing her little shorts, white slippers, and a pink top. Her hands were going everywhere as she tried to reach the shelves to pick up items she didn't even know; they just looked appealing to her. As I pushed the shopping cart down the center of the aisle, a lady came walking up the aisle past us. Just before she passed, Kiki tapped the woman on the shoulder and said, "Lady, weh you man deh?" I looked at the woman with shock and laughter. The woman laughed, and I apologized for what Kiki said.

I knew then and there that she wasn't a normal child. She had potential, and she would do great things. She had a spunk that no normal two- or three-year-old child had. The signs were always there as she would do little things at home that made me ponder and smile. For this reason, I also decided to start her off early in kindergarten.

She started out at the We Kids Kindergarten School. Her teacher was a lovely and kind woman, the principal too. Her teacher would wash and change her when she made a mess. Kiki was shy at first, so she didn't talk much and would do as most babies do when in an environment that was new to them.

Her first day was tearful for me. She dressed in her little blue and gray uniform, pink lunch bag, and backpack with one book and a few giant pencils and crayons. She was excited about school for the first few days until she realized that she would be away from home more and more; she started to cry after me but quickly stopped after getting used to everyone. It was a joy to see her off each morning and to pick her up. Even when her taxi driver would pick her up, I would tell the driver to pick me up as I would accompany him to get her.

I later moved her to another school, Tender Hearts kindergarten, as it was closer to my home, and I would have easy access to drop her off and pick her up. I also liked the philosophy of the school; they believed that every child could learn with the right training. It was also a Christian school. Kiki excelled at this school, and here, she also met her first best friend. She was a star in her own rights at this school. She would always wear her best outfits every Friday. This was the dress-down day in the school, a fun day for most kids as they would wind down after lunch and play games sometimes. She learned so many songs and would come home and teach everyone who would listen to them. One of the songs was about Naaman in the Bible, who had leprosy. There is a part of the song where she would do the dance showing how Naaman dipped in the Jordan to cleanse his leprosy. The story is in 2 Kings chapter 5 of the Bible. Boy, did she love this song and dance. I would laugh as she sang and danced for the family. She also had a school boyfriend named Julius. The principal told me that Kiki had a boyfriend, and I laughed so hard as she told me of a dilemma that happened where they both were jealous of each other (if I remember correctly). He was an Indian boy who later moved away and had to leave the school. She continued to grow in this school and became smarter. Her penmanship was stellar. I could not write like she did, and I was a proud mom. She had a problem with reading 100 percent, and I had to enlist the help of a staff member, whom the kids called Aunty Romaine, to help her. I had her repeat the last grade because she was born after the school year, and getting her into primary school before reaching the proper age would be hard (this was a thing in our country). I also did not want her to move on and to struggle as I did when I was younger, as I was a slow learner when I started out. She did improve a whole lot and graduated the following year with lots of awards and was also the salutatorian at graduation.

Since the age of two, she has been having a birthday celebration. She loved it when it was her birthday. At one time, I had to have two celebrations for her, one at her school and one at home. She wanted to celebrate with her friends, so I had to take ice cream and cake to her school. The children sang her happy birthday, and they all ate and had a merry time. She loved this kind of thing, sharing and seeing others happy. She would always ask her grandfather, who was living in New York at the time, to send her things. Whenever she would ask for things, be it games, toys, shoes, or clothes, she would ask for her cousins and all her friends as well. She didn't ask only for herself. This is the kind of person Kiki is. Loving, free-spirited, and kind. She would take all she had and give it away, not thinking how or who would replace it. She thought about everyone and would put their needs ahead of hers, except for when it came to eating bananas and oranges.

At eighteen months old, her father died. She didn't understand much of it, but it affected her at school. The principal at the kindergarten called me one day to say that she was crying. The reason was she saw the other children's fathers picking them up, and she started questioning how come her dad didn't pick her up. This brought tears to my eyes as I tried to explain to her that her father had died. I was heartbroken for her and wished she would get to experience a father's affection and, as she got older, a father's disciplinarian style (something about a father that when he speaks, everyone listens). She struggled with not having her dad for years and would sometimes ask questions about him. I tried to comfort her the best way I knew how. She was always a happy child and would bounce back really quickly. She was surrounded by people who loved her and loved her spirit. This helped her to overcome those younger stages of her life. She also loved God and would be in church every Sunday.

Kiki was and still is a child that was loved and wanted. I didn't know it then, but she has saved me in so many ways without even knowing. She became my hope when I had none, my reason for trying, for fighting, for being. She pushed me to be a better person, especially as a single mother. I prayed for her before I met her, and like most parents do before their child is born or even conceived, I had plans for her. This reminds me of how God has a plan for each and every one of us. Rich or poor, saved or unsaved, believer or not. Whether we want to accept Him or not, Christ died for us. This was the plan that God had laid out before the foundations of the world were created. The all-knowing God set a plan, a road map for each and every one of us to follow, but many, even myself, missed it a lot of times and took wrong turns. These wrong turns cause detours, delays, setbacks, and even death. God has said in His Word, "For I know the thoughts that I think toward you, saith the LORD, thoughts of peace, and not of evil, to give you an expected end" (Jeremiah 29:11). He also said that if we are careful to follow the book of the law, in this case, the road map, which is our Bible, we shall make our way prosperous. Here is what the entire verse says in Joshua 1:8,

This book of the law shall not depart out of thy mouth; but thou shalt meditate therein day and night, that thou mayest observe to do according to all that is written therein: for then thou shalt make thy way prosperous, and then shalt thou have good success.

— Joshua 1:8

Just as how we as parents plan for our children, so does our Heavenly Father. Just as a parent corrects and guides their children, so does our Heavenly Father. Just as children are disobedient to their parents, so are we disobedient to our Heavenly Father when we step out of His will and commands. When we do not follow the road map, we end up being lost and taking a path that was not designed for us. If God, who created you, has a plan for your life, why not ask Him about it. Save yourself the added trouble of fulfilling such a plan by asking; He'll show you. Without following what God says, our way will not be prosperous; we will not have that good success that He desires for us to have. Do not think of success as having material things only. Success is fulfilling your purpose in life. Joshua's purpose was to carry the children of Israel into the land God had promised them. He was to pick up where Moses left off. What promised land has God called you to conquer? Think about it, pray about it. If we do not rise to the occasion, many will be left behind; many will not find their path or get the help that they need to stay on that path and fulfill their purposes. Many depend on you fulfilling your purpose to push them into their purposes. Many depend on you fulfilling your purpose to help and save them. Think of your purpose as your true nature. I didn't know my purpose until I truly began to serve God. I had to meet Christ for the Holy Spirit to help me change my perspective, the perspective God wants me to have as He knows what He placed in me. It led me down this path, and I'm still growing. What if I never gave my life to Christ, what if I never truly served Him, what if I never overcame all the obstacles along the path of the road map and gave in to fear and lies from the enemy? What if I give in to future obstacles and accept defeat? I'll let you answer that.

I read some time ago in a book by the late great Dr. Myles Munroe that "our potential is so hidden in God that we have to seek him to find it." It is by seeking God that we realize our potential, and God gives us the power, strength, and understanding to materialize it. We also build on such potential as we are not to limit God to our last success or victory. God loves us so much that He sent His only begotten son, Jesus Christ, to die for us. He longs to show us who we truly are, not what others say about us or even what you think of yourself, as this might not be true. The only way to fulfill our purposes is by seeking the Creator of our souls. I want to serve my purpose. I want my child to serve her purpose. I want everyone reading this book to serve their purposes. How about you?

As I planned for my daughter, so too, God had a plan for her, and if I am not connected to God, I too can cause my child to miss the path on the road map for her life. So many times, I see parents allowing their little children to dictate to them that they don't feel like they are who they're supposed to be, and they want to dress like a girl or a boy. These things happen when we don't know God as Father. God created us in His image. He had a plan, and He brought that plan to life. Male and female, He created us.

> *And God said, Let us make man in our image, after our likeness: and let them have dominion over the fish of the sea, and over the fowl of the air, and over the cattle, and over all the earth, and over every creeping thing that creepeth upon the earth. So God created man in his own image, in the image of God created he him; male and female created he them.*
>
> — Genesis 1:26–27

This was how God created us, male and female, with dominion. I can't say that I feel like a boy, so I should dress like one. It's like saying to God that we don't like ourselves or asking, "Why did You give me this body?" Can a bedspread say I don't want to be a bedspread anymore; I want to be a pillow? We are to fulfill our purposes through seeking God and knowing Him. Follow the road map He designed for your life. There are so many testimonies of persons who were one way, and after meeting Christ, they then became who they were created to be. I love this line from the movie *The Chosen* where Mary Magdalene (who was filled with seven devils) stated after meeting Jesus and was delivered that "she was one way and now she is another." That is the power of Christ to transform lives. The devil wants to reassign our destinies, our purposes. He wants to confuse us and get us off track. Why? Because this means victory for him. If we are so lost, consumed in our grief and problems, or worldly lifestyle, we won't have time to seek God or even believe that He can help us by showing us a better way. There was a time when my child said to me that she didn't know if she liked girls. What did I do? Pray, pray, pray. I will not allow the enemy to rob her. To rob the world of what God will have her do. I got to understand that she was associating with a young girl who was lost and didn't know who she was. Spirits can transfer, and spirits can manipulate. I had to pray, pray, pray, and when necessary, fast and use the principles found in God's Word concerning us as His children. She does not feel that way anymore. God didn't make any mistake when He created us; sin corrupted us. As parents, we have to know what God is saying about our children, though we might not get the big picture or understand it all. The devil wants them, and we cannot openly hand them over to him. Just as a parent knowingly leaves her child with a neighbor who is a terror to children. God has a plan for us, and so does the devil. Which will you rather heed to?

I say all this to say that, without God, I could not have made it with my daughter. This is only the beginning of the fight for our lives and that of our children. I salute those praying mothers. Keep fighting because when it looks like nothing is happening, the enemy is slowly being beaten. One day you will not see the same struggles as before; that's because you never gave up fighting. There was a time that I did give up, but as you read on, you'll see. Just know that giving up is not an option when you are in a fight for your life and that of your child or children. Retreating means more destruction and even death.

Push on, mothers and fathers. Pray for your young ones daily. You can't even imagine half the things that the enemy tries to slip into their minds/thoughts to distort their views and confuse them. Pray! Learn all you can about prayers; Jesus gave us the model for prayer in Matthew 6. Your life must be surrendered to Christ if you want true and lasting success or healing. It might not come in a way you think or expect, but God does answer prayers. Don't despise the little breakthroughs you receive; give thanks and keep praying. Being thankful is also a key to breakthrough. Appreciate the fights, the tantrums, the scary situations because when the victory comes, you'll know it was your Father answering your prayers and showing that He cares and that He can. The hard times really teach us about ourselves and who God is if we have eyes to see and understand what is happening in the realm of the spirit.

The Promise

When Kiki was in the womb, I made a promise to God that she would serve Him; even when I wasn't at church, she would be there. I wasn't a child of God then (I was a backslider). I believed in Jesus but didn't accept Him as Lord of my life as yet. There is a difference. Many of us believe in God but have not accepted Christ. We cannot be a child of God if we have not accepted Jesus Christ. I believe in the Word of God, the Holy Bible. Parts of which the Jewish nation accepts as the Torah, and the other books after the Pentateuch, they do not recognize. But the Word of God says in John 14:6, "Jesus saith unto him, I am the way, the truth, and the life: no man cometh unto the Father, but by me." The Bible also states that "For all have sinned, and come short of the glory of God" (Romans 3:23). So, without confessing my sins and accepting Christ as Savior and Lord, I'm a sinner. "For with the heart man believeth unto righteousness; and with the mouth confession is made unto salvation" (Romans 10:10). Without Christ, we cannot see the Father. Gone are the days when God only spoke by the prophets; now, He can speak to you too if you believe. I love this particular story in the Bible about the woman at the well.

Our fathers worshipped in this mountain; and ye say, that in Jerusalem is the place where men ought to worship. Jesus saith unto her, Woman, believe me, the

hour cometh, when ye shall neither in this mountain,
nor yet at Jerusalem, worship the Father. Ye worship
ye know not what: we know what we worship: for
salvation is of the Jews. But the hour cometh, and
now is, when the true worshippers shall worship the
Father in spirit and in truth: for the Father seeketh
such to worship him. God is a Spirit: and they that
worship him must worship him in spirit and in truth.
The woman saith unto him, I know that Messias
cometh, which is called Christ: when he is come, he
will tell us all things. Jesus saith unto her, I that speak
unto thee am he.

— John 4:20–26

We must worship the Father in spirit and in truth. Many persons may not believe in Jesus Christ, but because of what He did on the cross by dying for my sins, me a wretched sinner, me that wasn't even born yet, me that He knew would or would not believe in Him but He died for me anyway, believing that I would come to Him. How can I let Him down? How can I not serve Him? After all, He knew me before I was knitted in my mother's womb. "I was cast upon thee from the womb: thou art my God from my mother's belly" (Psalm 22:10). Yet He died for me, yet He loved me.

While Kiki was in my womb, I prayed over her and told the Lord that, like Hannah, Samuel's mother (the story of Samuel in the Book of Samuel), I give her unto You. I don't know why I prayed that prayer; I wasn't living for God then, but I believe God had a plan. One that I didn't know then, but as time went on, it became clearer. I was so adamant in my thoughts about sending her to church even if I wasn't going. I decided that my child would serve God and that I would be there to help her. As time went on and she was able to speak clearly and use the restroom, I started sending her to church. I would send my daughter to church with a neighbor, take her myself and pick her up, or have her uncle do it for me. I was serious about keeping to what I told God that I would do. I didn't ask for anything, only that I wanted my child to live for God. Ultimately it would be her choice because God gave us free will, but I would be there to correct and show her the way.

I wish I had someone to show me the way when I was younger. To help me see what I knew that I needed. I knew I loved God and wanted to serve Him, but I didn't know how. No one in my family was actively seeking God. They knew of Him but didn't know Him. Yes, there's a God, but have we ever thought to seek Him? To say, "Hey God, why am I here? What is my purpose? What can I do for You?" Aside from someone inviting you to church, that's probably the only time some of us remember God. So-called Christians do it too. Only remember God whenever there's a service at church or when there is a need. Whilst at home or work, they carry on as if they are enemies with God by indulging in activities that gratify the flesh.

I have always loved God and went to church as a child. I gave my heart to Him at the age of ten or eleven. I remember going to church when I only had two dresses. I would rotate these dresses until one got shorter and left me with one. I remember it clearly. It was a green and black dress. The top had a stretchy material, and the bottom was green satin-like material. This dress later ripped around the waist, and I sewed it back together until I couldn't wear it anymore. I was at every service during the week and twice on Sundays. One lady whom I knew from my old community where I used to live offered to buy me a hat (beret) to wear to church. As I got older, I wondered if the hat was so important that she failed to see what I really needed. I was only ten or eleven years old. My mother didn't mind me going to church but what troubled me as I got older was how the church folks didn't pay any attention to me. I would walk home by myself at night, except for two times, as I remember, when they offered to take me on the church bus.

There were times when I would go to church with my grandmother and other times to crusades with the neighbors. I would walk until I lost the heel of my shoe. Yes, I was living in the country, lots of walking. In those days, a person had to have church clothes and shoes to wear to church, so when I didn't have what to wear, I stopped going, but there was a longing in my heart. I don't think my mother really cared if I went to church or not because she wasn't going, and therefore, she didn't buy me anything to wear. I remember that I would take an old bathtub that was at the side of the house and play church. I would get an old broomstick and run the stick through the hole of the tub and lean it up in a way to make it look like a podium with a mike stand. Then I would get my Bible and pretend as if there was an audience and preach to them. This was my fun.

Thank God that He sees the heart and does not see as man sees,

*But the LORD said unto Samuel, Look not on his
countenance, or on the height of his stature; because
I have refused him: for the LORD seeth not as man
seeth; for man looketh on the outward appearance, but
the LORD looketh on the heart.*

— 1 Samuel 16:7

Today we can go to church dressed casually, which is okay, but I do prefer to dress as if I'm going to church; that's just me. As I got older, I quit going to church, not because I wanted to, but lacked guidance. My mother wasn't a Christian; what could she teach me? I was on my own. There was no one; where was the church the Bible spoke about? Where was the church that baptized me? I was worse than before I became a Christian. I would curse, which I never did before, talk back, unruly in a sense. There was no one to help me or guide me as a child. I turned from God, but never fully; God was always on my mind. (How many of us have God on our minds but still do not serve Him?)

As a young adult, I would still pray and always think of God, but not live as He would want me to. I would visit church on Sundays. By this time, it was a different church than what I was used to or where I got baptized. The church where I first got baptized seemed like all they wanted to do was to baptize people but not care about them. Almost everyone in this church dressed well and wore hats. At the new church I started attending, people cared about your spiritual need as well as your physical need, and I felt at home. It was not filled with religion but the spirit of the Living God. No one looked down on you, and if they did, you didn't feel it. A note to those in the church, pay attention to those who don't look like you, dress like you, or even speak like you; remember, God looks at the heart.

People need guidance, a way to the light. If the church cannot see this, then some of these people will be lost totally. You could have the opportunity to nurture a bishop or an apostle, a musician, a life coach, etc., but your pride prevents you. Be careful; less when you think you stand, you fall. You might even entertain angels unaware; what will they report to God about you? Don't let religion limit you, step away from religiosity and follow the spirit of God. If someone is in need in the body of Christ and you don't see it or sense it in the spirit, check yourself. God uses us, human beings, to help others. So, if you're not doing your part, you are lacking. How are the unsaved supposed to see Christ in us if we ourselves lack Christ, lack the very nature of Him?

We are malnourished without a true relationship with Christ, the Savior. People can become so caught up in religion and culture that they fail to see or understand what the Spirit of God really desires of us, His children. Let us do all things as unto the Lord so that our calling and election will be sure. We must aspire to be like Christ, though our rising may be because of the things we go through or endure. The end goal is to be like Christ, not what culture, race, or ethnicity has said. How are we like Christ when we fail to cater to the needs of those in need? Look around; they are right beside you.

Though I had not turned back fully to God, I knew within that I couldn't fight to surrender forever. There was always a longing to see Him, to serve Him. Though I didn't understand, this was Him calling me all this time, but I didn't understand it. I did not know how to do it. I had a life to live, God was a part of it, but truly He wasn't. Everything I did was not centered around Him. It was centered around my sinful nature, pleasing myself. But I encourage you today that if you hear Him, harden not your hearts (Hebrews 3:7–8). My fight would not be victorious without Christ. As a matter of fact, no fight is victorious without Christ.

There is a war going on for our souls. Our children need the prayers of a righteous person. The Word of God says that the prayers of a righteous man are heard. "The LORD is far from the wicked: but he heareth the prayer of the righteous" (Proverbs 15:29). If the Lord is far from the wicked, what makes us think that He will hear our prayers when we are wicked? The only prayer that He will hear is one of repentance. That is what will get His attention. If we are not serving God the right way and praying for our children, it is not effective based on this word. Though God is gracious and kind, there is so much more that could benefit us if we are serving Him the right way. It was not enough for me to send my child to church or desire that she serve God. I had to decide that I would do right by God and my child as well.

There are times when God needs to work on us, the parents, first for the blessing to flow onto our children. It all starts at the head. Fix the head, and the body will come in alignment. It's not fair to desire the good things from God but be unwilling to serve Him. How dare I ask my boss for a raise when I'm always late for work, leave early, and have more than acceptable absences. Same thing with God. I cannot ask God for blessings on my child when I would not even give myself to Him fully. God wants all or nothing with us. He wants our hurt, our mistakes and failures, the good and the bad. He wants everything. When He is through with us, we will not be the same as those who He loves, He corrects. If we give ourselves to allowing Him to correct us and to work on us, many will wonder what happened to the person that they knew before; you're not the same in spirit; God has done something marvelous in you. I thank God for the day I said yes to all the hurt and pain, yes to the challenges, yes to the brokenness, yes to the fights with my child, yes to the sleepless nights. Yes, to His plans and purpose for my life. It did something wonderful for my daughter and still is today.

There is a saying that my fellow countrymen would say, "Whenever you're trying to do right, here comes the devil to mess you up." I believe this is true as the devil does not care so much about those who are already under his clutches. It is those who are actively serving God he tries to afflict, and that is why as believers, we are to hold fast to Christ because the enemy will try everything to get us off track.

As the chapter states, "The Promise," I am reminded of how many of us, at some time or the other, have made a promise or two to God. Whether it was a promise to change our lifestyle, stop smoking/drinking, stop swearing, stop beating a spouse, stop watching a particular TV show, etc., but somehow, we find ourselves doing the very thing that we promised not to do. There are some promises/vows that take careful consideration before committing to them. The Word of God says in

Ecclesiastes 5:4, "When thou vowest a vow unto God, defer not to pay it; for he hath no pleasure in fools: pay that which thou hast vowed." Wow, I am considered a fool if I fail to pay that vow. The next verse goes on to say that it is better not to have vowed than to vow and not pay. Deuteronomy 23:21 also states, "When thou shalt vow a vow unto the LORD thy God, thou shalt not slack to pay it: for the LORD thy God will surely require it of thee; and it would be sin in thee."

Failing to fulfill my promise to God is a sin, and that is another reason for me to continue praying for my daughter. I do not want to sin against God. I did my part by ensuring her spiritual needs were being met, and I'm still fighting for her. Imagine having your only child and seeing them suffer; what would you do? Imagine having a few children, and you cannot provide for them. Imagine seeing a ravenous animal running after your child; what would you do? You would do no different than what God has already done for us. He sent Jesus, the way, the truth, and the life. But we have to do our part in believing, in accepting His free gift of salvation.

Now imagine you calling out to your child, seeing that ravenous animal prowling and running to them, but the child is oblivious to what is about to happen; they don't even hear you calling. You yell and yell and run after that animal. Still, the child does not hear; they are distracted. The same way Jesus is calling us today, the devil is on the prowl, but we don't see; how can we see when the devil has blinded our eyes to his trickery? Jesus is fighting for us, but we don't even recognize or understand. I know that He is fighting for me; He showed me years ago that He is. I was not sleeping, but my eyes were closed, and I could see outside my window at the side of my house. There were angels and demons fighting. I could hear the swords clanging, and I thought to myself, *My God, what a vision.* God is always fighting for us though we do not see or know that there is an actual battle going on. This battle is for our souls.

In the same way, Jesus is chasing after you, to help you, to save you; all we have to do is look around. Stop letting the cares of life distract us from the true meaning of our existence. Let us seek to honor God in all our doing. As parents, we *must* pray for our children and the children of the world. Things became clearer to me as I built a consistent prayer life. Things I saw spiritually that would not be visible physically. Who can it be but God? Now imagine if I never fulfilled my promise. What happened next probably would not have happened, or at least, when it did.

Total Surrender

It came to the point where I decided that enough was enough. I stopped running and surrendered to God, to Jesus Christ. Things got harder for me, but I was always able to manage. I started attending church fully and totally surrendered my life to God, not because life was hard, but because I feared death. I didn't want to die, let alone die in sin. When I started going to church with Kiki, she was so happy, and I believed she shined even more.

Months later, I decided to rebaptize on my own will since the first one was forced by an altar worker. I surrendered my whole heart to God and never looked back. Though it was not easy, I failed a lot and messed up a lot, but I would pick myself up again and start over until I finally got it and learned how to keep standing, even in great trials. (Baptism should be a person's own choice, not something that is forced. The individual has to decide for themselves if they want Jesus or not; God gave us free will. Though we all need guidance to Christ, it should not be forced.)

The day came when Kiki said to me, "Mommy, I want to get baptized."

I was so happy to hear this, but I told her that she was too young. I was not ready for her to get baptized, but the response she gave me blew me away. Imagine, she was just seven years old at the time. I asked her, "Why do you want to get baptized?"

"I love Jesus in my heart, and I don't want to die," replied Kiki.

This pierced my soul; how could I say no? And that same year, she was baptized, accepting Jesus Christ as her Lord and Savior.

Her decision came not because I forced it or asked her to; this was God now answering a prayer that I had prayed years before. This was as a result of me allowing God to work through me, fixing the head, then the body. Fixing the head and working on the rest is a long process. Many failures and setbacks are in the process of fixing, but for the person who sticks with the process and allows God to work, then it will happen in their favor. One thing I was taught was that if Jesus is in the vessel with me, then I can ride out any storm. We must ensure that Christ is in the boat/ship with us today because if He is not, there will be loss. It is detrimental for any person going through a difficult situation without Christ. Though the pressures of life might ease sometimes, we need long-lasting release and deliverance. That only comes through Jesus.

I remember the day that she got saved. It was a sunny Sunday morning. There was Sunday school where the Word of God is taught, the welcome of guests and members, then the praise and worship team did their thing. This was then followed by the baptismal service. All those who had previously said yes to Jesus went to a room in the back to change, women on one side and men on the opposite side of the building. My baby girl changed into her leggings and T-shirt with her head covered to prevent it from getting wet. It was such a joy to see the little skinny girl walking up to the platform to say, "Yes, I believe that Jesus came to die for my sins." I was very elated and overjoyed. The praise team sang a host of songs based on the meaning of baptism, such as "Good-bye World, I Stay No Longer With You." Praises were up, and the angels in heaven rejoiced as she said, "Yes Lord, I am Yours."

Whenever a soul comes to the knowledge of Christ, the angels in heaven rejoice. Why? Because God has reclaimed what is His (Luke 15:10). He does not force Himself on us, so when we come to Him, He is super elated. Just like the prodigal son who returned to his father's house. The father saw his son coming from a far-off and ran to meet him, kiss him on the neck, put a ring on his finger, put the best robe upon him and a shoe on his feet, and made a feast for him. Why? His son, who was lost, is now found. His son, who was dead, is now alive. So does our Heavenly Father welcome us back, clean us up, and rejoice over our return (Luke 15:11–24). We are dead without Christ, and when we come to God, we are made alive. Here begins a new life. We surrendered to God.

It is a privilege to say yes to Christ. He endured the cross for us to come to the day where we'll be reconnected with our Maker. Coming to Christ does not mean that everything will be perfect after. Far from it. There will be seasons of testing and trials, many failures, or even backslidings in some cases. The Bible says in Romans 2:4 (NIV), "Or do you show contempt for the riches of his kindness, forbearance and patience, not realizing that God's kindness is intended to lead you to repentance?" What this is simply saying is that God is the righteous Judge, and we should leave all judgment to Him. He is the One who gives us time in our messes to change, to repent. His kindness and patience towards us should lead us to repentance, not to continue in our mess. As children of God, we need to repent. Repent from faulty mindsets and let God work on us.

My aim is to try and break it down for everyone to understand where I'm going and to see the end process, also how the wrong mindset can cause major damage. Like everything in life, we have to follow steps and let the process run its course. There is no skipping in the process, as what we don't master will master us. I've surrendered to God, or so I thought. I was going to church, very much involved as the Sunday school's secretary, doing good. Years later, I realized that I did not totally surrender to God. My faulty mindset caused me to handle pressure in a negative way. God had to really break me to build me up. Many times, we might run or want to run from the breaking process, but as I said, whatever we don't master will master us. My situation was mastering me. I was not totally surrendered to God. If I was, I would not have backslidden in my thoughts, in my attitude, in my belief in God, in my body. During the breaking, I was able to see my error. My mindset was messed up.

Religion can also mess up a person's mind, controlling their thoughts which leads to a faulty perception. If a person is going to church, active, is doing what they know is right such as reading their Bibles and praying every day. They call that serving God. What if I shall say that serving God is so much more than mere regiment according to the church. Serving God encompasses all these things, but if there is no real relationship with the Word of God, with the Holy Spirit, with Christ, then we are not truly serving God. If we are truly serving God, a sister in need will not continue to be in need. A brother in need would not continue to be in need. Here's why: it would be revealed as to what to do unless God is taking the individual through a process.

Truly serving God is walking in our purposes, not just keeping the seats of the church building warmed. We are to get up and do what God has created us for, and it all begins with true surrender, a changed mindset, and allowing the Word, the Holy Spirit, and Christ to work in us through our continued relationship and fellowship. Understanding this was when I truly, totally surrendered to God. Now I do things differently, and as you read, you'll see some of what I did out of ignorance and disbelief in the God that I serve.

Throughout my life, one of the things that the Lord always says to me is to trust Him. I believe that I was not truly trusting God because He had to remind me to trust Him. I would believe and trust Him for a season, and when a bigger problem or test comes, I relapse, not remembering what God had done before. God has not changed and what He requires is total surrender from all of us to trust Him in the small and big challenges. Each time God will stretch us a little more, and we ought to remember that He is still God, and if He did it before, He could do it again. When the situation comes, it always seems so hard, so tough to handle, but we are not to handle it. We are to do what God says in His Word. Pray, praise, worship, fast, give thanks, honor God and men, and do what He said in His promises. Here is the word "longsuffering." "The Lord is not slack concerning his promise, as some men count slackness; but is longsuffering to us-ward, not willing that any should perish, but that all should come to repentance" (2 Peter 3:9).

Longsuffering: this expression is made up of two Hebrew words, *arek* = "slow" and *aph* = "anger." Hence, "slow to anger." God is not easily irritated. The former two characteristics lead Him to lengthen out the offers of His mercy rather than punish immediately and wait to be gracious rather than to destroy. So "the longsuffering of God waited in the days of Noah, while the ark was being prepared." Under these conditions, when judgment finally comes, it is perfectly considered and just.

God is waiting on us to change, to repent. Repentance is not just for the sinners. Christians need to repent. Some of us who call ourselves Christians are even worse than those who are not. God is waiting, and when He begins to judge, who can stand it? Christ, the righteous Judge, gave His life for us, yet we take it lightly. We have no idea of the unseen realm that carries out its evil against humankind, even using humankind (occult) to assist in their wicked plans.

God is not slack concerning anything He has told us. We are the ones who slow up the process sometimes because our minds have not been renewed. Repentance does not stop at accepting Christ. It continues as we work on ourselves. As God shows us what and where we need to improve and we allow the Word of God to work by being practical, this is total surrender, when nothing moves you because you know the God whom you serve. Many times God repented of the evil that He would do to the children of Israel. The examples in Exodus, chapter 32, and Jonah, chapter 3, give a clear definition of what it means to repent. The children of Israel sinned against

God, and He wanted to destroy them, but then Moses interceded for the people, and God repented of the evil that He would do unto them. Remember, God wants to do good unto us, and He cannot pour out into an unclean vessel. We have to first change our thinking. We are to think of God's goodness towards us and know that He can do anything for those whom He loves, and He loves all of us. That is why He wants us to remember Him, to surrender to Him. Only a true believer will understand what it really means to surrender. If a person has to question if they have surrendered to God, maybe they haven't. If you know, you know. We need to surrender in every area of our lives for all things to flow freely and effectively. A surrendered heart sees God in everything.

The Unexplained Situation

As I said before, coming to God does not mean that our problems will automatically vanish. It will seem more like they increase. There were trials and trials in our lives. My feeble mind didn't understand what to do, and I coped the best way I knew how. I did not fully understand how to deal with the situation, and I was also unlearned.

For her, it began in kindergarten, at least the physical aspect of the problem, as it had started long ago in the spiritual realm. One day her teacher called me from school saying she was crying that her leg was hurting her. I took her to the doctor, but nothing came of it. Here began the issue of the unexplained pain in the leg. She would get up to get ready for school and could not walk on one foot. The knee could not bend; whenever she tried to, it would hurt. We did an x-ray, blood tests, and another test that I can't recall the name of it. All of which came back inconclusive; no one could figure out what was happening with her leg. This would occur a few times a year, but she insisted on going to school. She did not want to stay home. I took her to a fasting service at my church one day, and the prayer team and I prayed and anointed the leg. She had two to three more flare-ups after this. I would still pray but didn't know the proper way to pray for that situation.

There are prayers and different levels of prayers that are for specific circumstances. Then there are also certain keys and principles in the Bible that one must fulfill to attain results, although some results take a longer time. One thing that I know about prayer is that if I am praying for a miracle, I must be ready to deal with it and be able to maintain it. Therefore, it is good to look within our own lives and ask the Lord to deal with our hearts. Not that we might be the cause of the problem we face, but we live in a fallen world, and the more we understand our different situations, the better we are in prayer and better able to get results.

Throughout all this, she was still optimistic and filled with joy. She was the life of the house, our little entertainer. I remember one night, the electricity went out, and she decided that she was going to do a show for us (myself, her grandmother, aunt, and cousin). She did a little drama for us that night, and we laughed until we cried. Thinking about it now, I smile with tears in my eyes. She loves family, and she loves to make us laugh and see us happy. Though she didn't always have the best approach to getting attention, she knew how to make us laugh. She came home from church one day and saw her grandmother frying chicken. I remember her calling her cousin to come and look at the chicken, "Tee, come and look pon the chicken in the pot, it looks good een." Off the bat, she started singing. Here, she created her chicken song, "A di scrumptious chicken inna (in a) my mouth." We all laughed as she went on and on dancing and singing.

Every time there was a flair-up with her leg, she would insist on still going to school. I had to take her to school, and then at lunch, a friend/schoolmate would help her. The teacher suggested keeping her home because she was hopping to move around and needed help, especially going to the restroom. I explained to her that she did not want to stay home, but I would keep her home for a day. Though she didn't want to, she stayed home and rested until she was able to walk better. With every flair-up, it would just disappear after a few days like nothing happened. This puzzled me for days, but I trusted God for a solution. Then it all just disappeared when she was between nine and ten. Call it a miracle, but whatever you might think it was, I knew God had her.

There will always be some kind of obstacle or challenge that we might face, which will be very difficult to bear or even understand, but we cannot lose hope in the God who saves us. A situation may take years before a breakthrough comes, but we must be relentless in our pursuit of seeking God no matter the challenge. Though I did not fully understand the scope of prayer, God, in His mercy, still acted because that's who He is. "It is of the LORD'S mercies that we are not consumed, because his compassions fail not" (Lamentations 3:22).

I don't know what your unexplained or perplexing situation is, but God does. The only way that we can have victory is to cry out to the all-knowing God who reigns in the heavens, who is the Lord of all. As parents, we send our children to school to learn, or we teach them at home so they can become fruitful and knowledgeable adults, not just to earn bread later in life. Likewise, we go to God to get knowledge to make us fruitful and prosperous. The things that are hidden in our lives, He can reveal. How? By spending time with Him. By reading our Bibles and books that teach about God and His ways. But the best book is the Bible.

Later in my journey with God, I began to understand and see things differently. This is God revealing Himself to me. Why? Because I chose to spend time with Him. I chose to read and learn all that I could, and I'm still in the school of knowledge. Reading and spending time with God is an everyday practice and should be done every day. Don't we eat every day? Yes. So, as children of the Most High, we need the filling only God can give daily.

Many of us take up God every other day or only on a particular day. Do you think that the devil only comes at us some days? Do you think that the problems we face are playing with us? We need to stop playing with God and racking up points with the devil. I've heard of Christians who only attend church every other Sunday. Why? Because in their mind, they don't need to go every Sunday; since they went the Sunday prior, they don't need to go the Sunday after. This is a faulty mindset. A stronghold set up by the evil one. How do I know? I've lived that life when I was in the world. I only visited church every other Sunday. That is a worldly mindset. To fellowship does not mean one has to be in a physical building as long as there is a place and time for active and continual fellowship. We need to unlearn some ways of our forefathers that were sealed in culture and beliefs. Ask what God says now about a matter.

Many of us are still walking with God in one hand and the devil in the other. We are not ready to die to ourselves, so the Lord cannot have His way because, as my sister in Christ, Nicolette, would put it, "Our hands are filled, so how can God put anything in it." Our hands are filled with baggage that God is saying to get rid of so I can help you. Help you with the perplexing situations, help you become who He has called you to be. Help you become less like you and more like Him. Help you break the outer man into walking in the spirit.

If this describes you, start again. Start with God, and whatever He says to do, do it. Though it will hurt, though it will inconvenience you, do it. The whole point is to know that it's not about you or me, it's about God and His will being done, and that includes freeing us totally from every weight of sin. But we must let go. Many of us are so unhappy because we fail to realize that it's not about us. God's perfect will must be done in our lives. We fight against the will of God and then blame God when we get burned, when things don't go the way we think they are to. Now can we fight against the will of the God who created us? We need to awaken and arise from our blindness. We are so foolish to the will of God for us; I know I was. I am not perfect; far from it, that is why I need His direction every day. We need His will for our lives to be all who He says we are. So let go. What are you holding on to today?

> *Therefore, since we are surrounded by such a huge crowd of witnesses to the life of faith, let us strip off every weight that slows us down, especially the sin that so easily trips us up. And let us run with endurance the race God has set before us.*
>
> — Hebrews 12:1 (NLT)

Let us let go and run the race that God has set before us. The one who endures to the end receives the prize.

Though this chapter is called "The Unexplained Situation," it is nothing new, and it can be explained. Problems from nowhere, warfare, troubles, and the likes are not new to anyone. It happens to the best of us. I just didn't understand the situation at first. What destroys God's people? We perish without the knowledge from above. We might even feel like we're living but slowly dying on the inside.

The trials also come to break our outer man. If we are to be effective in serving God, we must shed the outer man (our fleshy attitude) and walk in the Spirit (the inner man). Become one with the Spirit of God. I did not recognize that God wanted to break me to rebuild me. We do not know how or what God will do or allow for us to be broken into the masterpiece we are, but we must submit to the process and allow Jesus to take full control. When Christ has full control, our eyes will become open. The process will take years, and it won't always be pretty. It may seem unfamiliar, hard, and tough, but we must trust God and seek His guidance, whether in prayer, the Word, fasting, etc., in overcoming. There is a breakthrough with our names on it; first, allow the process to run its course and remain faithful and prayerful.

Bitter Sweet Migration and Living with My Dad

Fast forward to September 2015, when we moved to the US, I didn't tell her we were moving until a week before we left. I begged her not to tell anyone that we were leaving, but that was hard for her. Maybe I should've discussed the move with her more in depth on what was really happening. I was not thinking about how she would feel. I expected her to be happy about it; I didn't consider her feelings; after all, she was a child. What a sad way to think. It was her life too, and I was uprooting everything that she knew; she should have been more involved whether she understood the full scope of the move or not.

She struggled to accept that we were not going back home to Jamaica but only to visit. Her aunt and cousin did not move to the states until several months after we did. She missed them and missed having everyone all in the same place, in the same yard, as we called it. She now had her grandfather, my dad, close to her, but they weren't as close as the family whom she had left behind. She missed her friends and the ability to run next door to visit a friend or have her sleepovers. She loved inviting her friends over, and she would have sleepovers ever so often. Playing games with her friends, sharing stories, and watching Disney movies. Sometimes, I would take them to the beach and to church. This was all a part of her life. It was her fun, and she missed it.

She thought that moving to the US would be better than her birth homeland, but it was not. What she expected or had in mind turned out to be somewhat of a nightmare for her. She didn't have friends; she didn't have the support of her church community; she missed her grandmother and the perks of having her always doing things for her. This included making her favorite tea at night. When she was younger, she would always go to her whenever she couldn't have her way with me. She loved milk, and I'm not talking regular cow's milk but Lasco milk. It is a popular powdered milk in the Caribbean. One pack goes by so fast with her, and I would have to hide it from her. She would cry for this milk, and I would just pretend as if I was sleeping. Her "gram gram," as she would call her sometimes, would always come to the rescue, and then I would yell at her for making it.

Then there were times when her gram gram could not buy fruits such as bananas and left them on the countertop or on top of the refrigerator because by the time she came in from the market, and Kiki knew there were bananas, they would be almost gone by the evening. She used to say to me that Kiki must be a monkey the way she ate bananas. A hand/bunch would be on the table, and by the end of the day, two or three would be left for gram gram. I used to laugh whenever this happened because she was the one who was spoiling her. It got to the point where she was afraid to buy bananas, and when she did, she would start eating them right away to prevent her not getting any and hide the rest in a black plastic bag; of course, Kiki would find this too. I think she was watching around a corner or something to know the hiding spot because not even I knew the hiding spot.

She and her gram gram had a good relationship. From time to time, I would hear stories from my mother of what Kiki said to her or something she did when she thought no one was looking. My daughter was something else, and she still is. There are a lot of fond memories of who she is and the fun she brought to an empty family. I believe that having family around also brought out her personality.

Living with my dad and other siblings was not easy for both of us. For me, it felt like I was in prison, to be honest. Imagine how Kiki felt. The one person who should have her back and be there for her was now too busy to really enjoy her growth and understand the changes that were taking place with her. I had to figure out how to manage work, school, bills, and life overall. Although I was providing for her, I lacked communication with her and maintaining that emotional support that I was always able to give. I was dying and needed saving; I didn't see it happening to her. I was focusing on myself, not thinking that something like depression would affect her. I was working and in school. She was in school. I could get her some things that I couldn't before as I now had easier access to certain things; how did this happen? All of what I was doing didn't matter because she needed love and support and I was too caught up with myself to see that she needed me. I thought that I was trying to make it all the better for her. "Everything will be okay once I finish school and have a better job," is what I would say to her. Wrong!

I started college a year after moving to the United States. I was also working part-time. There was a lot of pressure in the house, too little space, and too many people talking. Like I said, I felt like I was in prison, and there was no support. I had a new church family; I started a two-year Bible college program as an extension of a particular Bible college that was offered at the church I was attending. I had no one really because everything and everyone was new to me. Though I would speak to my mother, she didn't know all of what I was going through, and I didn't want to worry her. I would speak to my spiritual mother. And though she would encourage me, and I would use the Word of God, I wasn't fully trusting what the Word of God said; I wasn't putting it into practice. I became dull; I sank more and more. I was on a roller coaster, sometimes up and sometimes down. My pastor's wife, Pastor Spencer, gave me a word from Philippians 4:6, "Be careful for nothing; but in everything by prayer and supplication with thanksgiving let your requests be made known unto God." I read it; I also knew the verse but didn't apply it until much later, which was too late by then. I believed in the Word but believing without application was useless. Faith without works is dead. "For as the body without the spirit is dead, so faith without works is dead also" (James 2:26).

All that I knew was now hard to put into practice. It was like I was in a tight hole with a pin-size breathing space. I was stifling both spiritually and physically. I was supposed to be the strong one for both of us, but I could not manage. (Remember, I said earlier, we are not to handle it to use the principles in God's Word. See the chapter "Total Surrender," page 21.) I was trying to manage on my own and not trusting God to do it for me.

> *Come unto me, all ye that labor and are heavy laden, and I will give you rest. Take my yoke upon you, and learn of me; for I am meek and lowly in heart: and ye shall find rest unto your souls. For my yoke is easy, and my burden is light.*
>
> — Matthew 11:28–30

Here is a principle that I failed to obey. Of course, I'm going to be burdened if I take on what I cannot carry or what was not meant for me to carry. When I was supposed to push, I relaxed. The moment I relaxed, the enemy won. But the fight was not over; the longsuffering and gracious Father was fighting for me still. I would fight back in God's strength, and after a while, I was able to stand somewhat. I was weak because I was drifting. The situation rocked me to the core, and I thought that there was no coming back. But God, the little wins, was God fighting for me, though I did not understand much of my situation as this was all new to me, and I had nowhere to turn, no one to help. No one had the experience and wisdom to help me.

What are we to do when we have nowhere (to go) and no one (to turn to)? This was when the Lord gave me Psalm 27:10, "When my father and my mother forsake me, then the LORD will take me up." Scriptures such as this were what kept me sane. Sometimes we don't know our strength until we are pushed to the limit. My strength failed me, and I was now walking in the strength of the Lord. It was an uphill battle that would last over two years.

I did not expect to feel the way I did nor experience the things that I did, but I believe God did what He could with what was given to Him. I wasn't doing my part in the relationship. I was supposed to be in prayer, in fasting (this dwindled as pressure hit me), and I was supposed to be in constant communication with Him to find strength, grace, mercy, and peace. I was supposed to be there for my girl, to love her, to hug her, to let her know that God loves us, to read to her, and to comfort her. I took my eyes off God and onto my problems. No one could understand me or what I was experiencing. I needed saving; I needed the saving and helping grace of God. I was fighting an internal battle. I needed God's people to rise up and care for the fatherless, the widow, the poor, etc., as His word says. But this fight was all on me. This was how I felt. But I was never alone; you see, God was always with me, though I could not feel Him, He was always there, and that is why I'm standing today, that is why I can say what I say in this writing. This is why I can declare,

> *I will be glad and rejoice in your unfailing love, for you have seen my troubles, and you care about the anguish of my soul. You have not handed me over to my enemies but have set me in a safe place.*
>
> — Psalm 31:7–8 (NLT)

In our trials and difficulties, we often feel alone and that maybe no one cares. We may seek help from mankind, but our help comes from God. At the same time, if God's people are not inclined or in-tune to His words in helping their brothers and sisters in Him, the strangers, and so on, they lack in the key area of helping. No one wants to be inconvenienced or out of place in helping others. What does the Word say? This is my go-to in answering such things. "When God's people are in need, be ready to help them. Always be eager to practice hospitality" (Romans 12:13, NLT). When was the last time we did this as God's people? Praying or asking a person in need how they are, does not suffice. Prayer is good, but oftentimes we pray for what God has already given us the answer to or directives on what to do. Read the Word! There are so many other scriptures I could add here on how we are to act in helping others. Sometimes my child will ask me something to which I have already given the answer. My response is almost always, "What did I tell you before? Try to remember," or "I told you already, I'm not going to tell you again." We must stop asking God what to do when He has already given us the answer. Read the Word!

On another note, some battles we have to go through on our own for God to break and rebuild us into His image and likeness. Some things about us are so flawed that it is only through the breaking and shaking, only through the fire, that we'll really learn and understand what God is doing, saying, and expects of us, His chosen people.

As people in the world, we are all given grace, but as we come to God, He gives us more grace. There are things we will not attain and come to the knowledge of if we still have a worldly mindset. Hence the shaking in our lives. Some shaking leads us to God; some cause us to drift, which is never the intention; it is always to come to God. Some shakings are so harsh that if God Himself does not fight for us, we are lost forever. Now I'm not saying that God will cause us to experience the worst, but He'll allow certain things to happen so it can lead us back to Him. Let your shakings and fiery trials lead you to the King and not the enemy. Do not seek the help of mediums and the like; this is witchcraft and bondage. You will never be free this way. The problem might be masked, but still there. Follow the Word of God.

> *Dear friends, don't be surprised at the fiery trials you are going through, as if something strange were happening to you. Instead, be very glad—for these trials make you partners with Christ in his suffering, so that you will have the wonderful joy of seeing his glory when it is revealed to all the world.*
>
> — 1 Peter 4:12–13 (NLT)

> *Wherein ye greatly rejoice, though now for a season, if need be, ye are in heaviness through manifold temptations: That the trial of your faith, being much more precious than of gold that perisheth, though it be tried with fire, might be found unto praise and honor and glory at the appearing of Jesus Christ.*
>
> — 1 Peter 1:6–7

We must fight the good fight of faith. In all things, we must give God thanks. Why? Because that is what He desires of us. We will never understand all things. Walk by faith and believe God for the unexpected, according to His Word and will for our lives. There is no victory in witchcraft. If you need lasting cure, lasting deliverance, eternal life, seek God.

It Gets Harder/
House of Torment

L iving with my father was not as I thought it would be. People do change, and living with people that you're not used to can be tough. One has to learn a person's ways and behavior and cope with it in the best way possible. My daughter was not used to the yelling and quarrels. There were a lot of them. After a while, it was like the house became toxic. Too toxic to even think right.

I started working a month after arriving in the US; a cousin helped me to get a job with a retail pharmacy. I worked my way up to becoming a supervisor, but it was not easy. A lot of sacrifices, working late, going in early, and not spending the time with my daughter that she needed. She was growing up right in front of me, and I didn't see it. I expected her to understand, to bear with me, to know that she is a child and she has to go along with what I say or do. She was supposed to be okay with what I was doing, trying to make a better life for us in our new country, "the land of opportunities," they call it. Man, was I wrong. Our story may not be the same as others, but this is what happened to us and, as time progressed, how we found hope.

After all the fuss and misunderstandings in the house, we basically got thrown out of the house we were living in, only it wasn't physically done. Where were we supposed to go with no one to turn to and nowhere to go? Living on your own in America is very hard, especially as an immigrant with no strong support, no friends, nothing. No one wants to rent a single bedroom to a parent with a child because there are other tenants in the house, and it's a shared space. Rent for a one-bedroom in New York was expensive and still is. I was only working part-time; even with full-time work, landlords requested tenants to be earning a certain amount. What were we supposed to do? I had nowhere to turn but to DHS.

We were placed in a shelter/transitional housing not too far from the area where we used to live. It was fine at first, but Kiki took it real hard. After realizing that we were living at a shelter, she became conscious of who was watching her walking to the building and if anyone would see her from her school, although the school was not close by. I was also careful not to let her feel ashamed or low in spirit because we now had to live where we were living, but I would encourage her that it would not be forever and one day we would be in our own place, and one day, own our own home. I would say, "Just give me some time." The funny thing was, I used to pass by the shelters without even knowing that; that's what it was. I remember passing by one on the train and looking ahead and saying to myself how I wished I was able to live in a building and have my window open, like the one I was looking at (be careful what you ask/wish for). To see light, to get fresh air. I felt locked up and in darkness where I was living. No one knew the internal battle that was going on within me. I put on a brave face, but no one knew. Can you imagine how Kiki felt? Children do experience different emotions and need emotional support. But how can you support someone if you're broken? What I didn't know was that God was testing me. He didn't put me where I was, but He allowed it. It was my response to the situation that prolonged the process.

Now don't feel bad or sorry for us; let our story bless and help you. Many of us will go through trying times and difficult situations, as mentioned in the previous chapter, but if we can remember whom we serve, we know that all things work together for our good. Why? Because we love God and we are called according to His purpose, according to Romans 8:28, "And we know that all things work together for good to them that love God, to them who are the called according to his purpose." If I didn't know that before, the trials taught me. Many people will run from their seasons of testing and seek the easy way out, not knowing that those who endure to the end shall receive the crown. The easy way out for me was to run off with a man who wanted to pay my rent in full for two years. I told myself that if this man could do it for two years, God could do the same and more for me. I chose God's way because what can a man do for me that God can't do? I was in the shelter for two years. God took care of my rent for two years, and I held my integrity.

Call me crazy, but I saw this as a blessing, even with everything that happened, because what I couldn't see was God working on my behalf and bringing me into the woman He created me to become. God knew that I could not afford the high rent, and no one wanted to rent a room to a stranger with a child, a one-room. The other thing was that my only cousin, who I knew would take us in, had moved to a new state three months earlier. She even told me to move down to where she was, but I was in school. So, I had to do what I did. This was God's way.

Imagine, I would have lived a shacked-up life with a man selling my soul just to have a roof over my head, but God offered another way out, and I took it. I would not have become who I am without the fiery trials and challenges or curveballs of life. I would not be writing this book which I hope will help many mothers and women by the grace of God. I chose God over man, and I will always choose God. What can a man do for me that the eternal, the Creator God cannot? Not a dang thing.

I remember when a rich man wanted to marry me, and I said no. Who wouldn't jump at this? I did not. This man was not who God had for me. His life was not right; he was a churchgoer. It never felt right in my spirit, and at the time, I wasn't even baptized yet. I was to be baptized two months later. The enemy sent a man from the church expecting me to say yes to him. The enemy wanted to shut me down with a man who was going nowhere. It was never about money for me. I really wanted God. It is God who giveth the power to gain wealth, "But thou shalt remember the LORD thy God: for it is he that giveth thee power to get wealth, that he may establish his covenant which he sware unto thy fathers, as it is this day" (Deuteronomy 8:18). How I do in the test will determine my altitude and how long I stay in the same season. I would encourage everyone to trust God and not give up during their testing; cry if you must, declare the law of God's Word, but do not give up. Know that God honors His Word, and if you're in the right standing with Him, God will move on your behalf. And if you do not know Jesus as Lord, get to know Him; certain things require a relationship with the Redeemer Christ.

After moving into the shelter, no one knew at first. I would tell my daughter not to let anyone know where we were staying. My nephew wanted to stay with us for a weekend, and I had to let him know that I was staying with someone. That was the story I used. I'm sure the family must have felt some type of way because no one knew where I was now living, but who wanted to advertise living in a transitional home?

Our room was a one-bedroom studio. We were comfortable for the most part. No one to bother us, the place was clean, and we had items that we needed to survive. The only side effect of living in a transitional home is there are random room inspections and signing in and out of the building, and I could not leave my daughter as she was under the approved age to be left on her own. I, however, had the best case manager, Ms. J; this was God's favor on me again. I had a previous case manager who wanted me to lie about something that I can't remember for me to get approved for housing. I told him that I didn't want him to lie for me and that I didn't agree with what he said to the rep on the phone. It was on more than one occasion that I felt that he was rude at times, and I requested a change in the case manager. He probably thought that I was into him because I invited him to church when I was only concerned about his soul; I wasn't looking for a man. He mentioned in a meeting with a supervisor how I invited him to church in a tone that would cause her to think I was coming on to the man. Anyway, I got the switch, and God knew I would. I believe this man could not have helped me in my situation with my daughter, and God knew I needed someone who was just right.

This woman was a woman of God. She made the time in the shelter so much better, and I give God thanks for her. No one is supposed to have certain things in a shelter like a microwave and other electronics. We, however, had every little thing to our comfort. All this was really to help Kiki feel like she was living a decent life and that she wouldn't feel so depressed. I do hope that DHS managers understand that some of the limitations that they have can be improved for the sake of the children. This was a family shelter. I do understand that when people get too comfortable, they do not want to seek every way possible to help themselves, but a little help for the children's sake can go a long way. Mental health disorders are no joke, and when we can prevent certain things, then we must do so. Depression does not happen overnight; it's a slow build-up until one day, *boom*! And like I said, I was not paying attention. The problem is that when the devil sees an opportunity to wreck us, he will pull out all the stops to do so. Trauma opens the door to depression and other mental health disorders. This is what the devil will capitalize on.

What is in your life or the life of your child or loved one that you are not giving full attention to? What we fail to address will only fester up until it cannot fester anymore, then we see or hear the big bang. Everything burst wide open like a dam. We all know what that can lead to, catastrophic damages. The Word says that we must be vigilant and that we are to always pray. Prayer helps us to hear what we wouldn't otherwise. This is also how we get spiritual intelligence. If I didn't love to pray before, I certainly do now.

Ms. J would ensure that Kiki was okay. She fought so hard for us to get an apartment, and when we finally did, she made a call to the rep and begged her to find us a good building and a nice community, and that the rep did. God knew what He was doing, and like I said, God didn't put me where I was, circumstances did, but He allowed it. If He wanted me to stay with a family member, He would have opened that door. If He wanted me to stay with a church sister, He would have opened that door. Trust God in all thy ways, acknowledge Him, and He will direct thy paths. "Trust in the LORD with all thine heart; and lean not unto thine own understanding. In all thy ways acknowledge him, and he shall direct thy paths" (Proverbs 3:5–6). Trust the way that God directs, no matter how difficult or foolish it seems. No matter what people say. One of the things that the Lord told me to do constantly was to pray for my child and those in the shelter. I wish I had listened and done more praying. I wish I was more obedient then. As I got closer to God, I realized that when He gives a command or tells me to do something, and I don't or do it partially, that's disobedience. Call it what it is and not make excuses or try to bargain with God.

Now the reason this chapter is called "House of Torment" is really to show how bad the shelter can be as well as how God delivered and can deliver in any situation. Like I said before, it also depends on our reaction, attitude, and behavior in or during the season of testing and trial. Living in transitional housing was alright for me, but not for Kiki. After a while, she began to change. Four or five months after living in transitional housing, I saw it. The onset of puberty and having to deal with it where she was. Puberty wrecked her mind emotionally, and this was where the devil came in. I was too busy with work and school. I ensured that she had all she needed, but what she really needed was my time and love. Some children, I believe, can do with little affection whilst others you have to give 110 percent. She was one who needed 110 percent. She started acting out, ACS became involved, and this was where the therapy started. Evaluations took place, nights at the hospitals when she was acting out, and I had to call the ambulance on a few occasions. One night it was so bad I could literally feel the devil taunting me. The police came with the ambulance, and it was not a pretty scene. This was when I told myself that I was going back to my country.

After careful consideration and speaking to her, she encouraged me not to give up, that she'll try to do better. She was trying, but this was something bigger than both of us; we needed Christ's redemptive power to work. It got to the point where I was missing school a lot, sleepless nights as she threatened to run away. To be honest, I gave up. I was so tired of the fighting I couldn't pray anymore. I believed in God, but I didn't want to pray. I couldn't; it was too hard. I read my Bible, but that was just out of mere religion or just to say I read. Then I stopped reading so often, and it became once in a while. The devil was winning, and I let him. I was trying to fight in my own strength, and therefore, I became tired. I didn't trust God fully. Why did He say I should pray? But I kept on doing things my way. It took me over two years to realize what I was doing and not doing. Don't let that be you. I knew the fight was spiritual, but I kept using things to appease her, and nothing worked. I'll show you why I know this fight is spiritual.

When she was a child, I saw some witches; only they didn't seem like it at the time. We were at a poolside, and then I saw a woman, I assume she was the leader, come up from under the water as shown in the Disney movie *Little Mermaid* when the king came up with his crown and scepter. This woman had a crown and a scepter in her hand. She asked me to give my daughter to her. I said, "No, I will not give my daughter to you; I can't give my daughter to you." She then turned and left. Secondly, the unknown pain in her leg that disappeared after much prayer. Also, one night I saw two witches enter our room at the shelter and sprinkle some powder-like substance on her bed. I could see her sleeping on the top bunk, and I was on the bottom, but I saw what had happened. I then said to them, "Oh, so it's you coming here doing this to make her behave like that." I was mentioning her behavior. The witches then turned on me and threw the same powdery substance in my face. I fell to the ground, weakened, and cried out for Jesus. Then I regained my strength and wiped my face. When one of them saw that I was now standing, she threw some more of the powder substance on me. I fell again, but only this time I did so under pretense for them to think I'm wounded or what they had done worked. I then saw them walk through the door and leave (the door was not open). I got up, ran to the bathroom, and washed my face. I woke up from the dream and anointed myself and my child, and prayed. Now, this is not to scare the faint-hearted or unbelieving but to open your eyes to the fact that there is a spiritual realm where devils and angels are. That we are fighting a spiritual warfare according to Ephesians 6:10–13,

> *Finally, my brethren, be strong in the Lord, and in the power of his might. Put on the whole armour of God, that ye may be able to stand against the wiles of the devil. For we wrestle not against flesh and blood, but against principalities, against powers, against the rulers of the darkness of this world, against spiritual wickedness in high places. Wherefore take unto you the whole armour of God, that ye may be able to withstand in the evil day, and having done all, to stand.*
>
> — Ephesians 6:10–13

Many will not understand this, you might call me crazy, but if you know, you know what I'm saying is true. Even those who are trying to help my daughter (doctors, therapists, etc.) don't even understand, so I just keep what I know to like-minded people, people who know God and are hungry for God. People who understand that God speaks through visions and dreams. This is how He shows us things to come as well as warns us, corrects us, gives directions, and so on. As long as I can remember, even before giving my life to God and accepting Jesus as my Lord and Savior, I have had dreams that come to pass. Only after living for Jesus do I understand better to pray when I get certain dreams and refute or come into agreement with my Papa. I am also still learning.

Then there was school trouble. I had to attend classes three days per week. Work and school, school and work, no social life, really. I would attend church outside of work and school and, once in a while, would go for lunch with a workmate who became a good friend. When I didn't know where to go, I would ask him for help. Like going to an office building that I didn't know, so he would tell me how to get there, then I started using google after getting to know my new surroundings. School life was hard. It was hard enough with all the papers and other assignments, then dealing with a child with depression on top of that was no walk in the park. It was okay for a while managing, but when it got tiring, I wanted to give up, and this was where she encouraged me to try and not to give up. She said, "Mommy, don't give up; you can do it." I was so proud of her for encouraging me in my distress while she had her own struggles.

Going forward, I had to let my professors know what I was dealing with if the situation warranted it, like missing more than two classes. I would still keep abreast of what was happening via classmates, posted assignments, and so on. Throughout all this, I was never late with an assignment and did every test or exam. I would study and do assignments or projects on days that she went to school or wasn't in a bad place/mood. I had to make good use of the good days, no matter how tired I was from work or school. Sometimes I would stay later after a class or go in earlier to get some work done. I did this for years. I was so relieved when it was finally over. Now I'm contemplating grad school, but the much-needed break is not over yet. I need more time to unwind and catch myself. I also need more time to draw closer to God and to my daughter.

School was hard for her too. She experienced bullying in middle school. This, added to moving again, was double pressure. She was not doing well in school. My honor roll daughter was in a bad place, and the devil was laughing. Parents need to understand that they *must* pray for their children daily. I had to set reminders sometimes to remember to pray because life was so busy. Not anymore do I do this as I became intentional about my prayer life. My friend and current pastor, Pastor Smith, as I believe him to be a divine connection God made years ago while we were in high school, would say to me and everyone, "Give God your time, and He will give you more time."

Parents, pray for your children. The devil desires to have them. If we could see the plans that the enemy has for them, we would not miss a day spending time praying for our children. Many times the Lord had me on rescue missions for our children, spiritually rescuing them from witches and warlocks, and as I write, I am reminded of why they attack me so. If I'm out of the way, they are free to ravage our children, but in the name of Jesus Christ, they will not have our children no matter how long or hard we fight in prayer, leaving it all in God's capable hands. I believe that we all have a calling, and each of us who knows our calling is to help those who don't. If we fail, we fail them. If I fail, I fail my child, plus other children, and I cannot let that happen.

As she moved on to high school, she began to find her place and understand better who she was. She made friends that faded after a while, except for one that remained. She once said that she needed friends that believed in God as she did. I do pray that she will find good Christian friends. Friends who are serious about serving God in spirit and truth. This is one of my prayers for her, but she also has a part to play for this to happen. She has to return to God with all her heart.

There are times when we want God to do things for us, but we have a role to play for God to move in the way we desire. Also, do our desires match that of God? Now, her desire is a good one but is she in the right standing with God to have this prayer answered? She once blamed God for what had happened and turned from Him. She has repented of it, but she has not fully returned to God. Like adults, we can't want certain things from God and not offer sacrifice. That sacrifice could be our time, money, obedience, service to others, etc. What are you blaming God for?

I could blame God for allowing me to move to a new country and experiencing all the negatives that we had experienced. I chose to thank Him and see that He is working on my behalf. I realized that I am not my own; it's not about me; who is me? If we can see the bigger picture, we will be better at it. It's not about me; it's about God's will, God's plan for mankind coming to fruition. Me, joining and agreeing with what God says about me and doing His will. My choices, attitude, and response to every situation affect the outcome, good or bad. Though hard it might be, we must try to see God in everything and pray about everything, giving thanks to God always. Even as I write these words, I can see why there are certain scriptures in the Bible, and my understanding of them is more illuminated because of my experiences.

I've heard of people blaming God for their demise, for the death of loved ones, and so on. Let me say that it only leads to bitterness of the soul and opens the door for the devil to afflict you. I watched a movie once where a couple was expecting a child, and the child died. Though the mother questioned God why, she couldn't understand why it had to happen to her. They were good Christians and did what God wanted. Let me say that no matter how good you think that you are, you are not exempt from trials, from problems. We live in a fallen world, and therefore, as children of God, we are not exempt from the afflictions of the world, but we have the answer to everything: Jesus. Now, the mother began to heal by looking at the bigger picture. If I remember correctly, she said that "God loved her unborn child so much that He needed him in heaven." Not long after, the mother became pregnant again and had her child. What if she had cursed God and complained? She would have failed her testing.

Father Abraham was willing to offer Isaac as a sacrifice to God. This was his testing, and he passed the test in Genesis 22:9–12,

> *And they came to the place which God had told him of;*
> *and Abraham built an altar there, and laid the wood*
> *in order, and bound Isaac his son, and laid him on the*
> *altar upon the wood. And Abraham stretched forth his*
> *hand, and took the knife to slay his son. And the angel*
> *of the LORD called unto him out of heaven, and said,*

Abraham, Abraham: and he said, Here am I. And he said, Lay not thine hand upon the lad, neither do thou anything unto him: for now I know that thou fearest God, seeing thou hast not withheld thy son, thine only son from me.

— Genesis 22:9–12

This was Abraham's testing to sacrifice his only son. Abraham did so willingly. He might have contemplated the act, but I imagine he believed that God could bring back his son to life and also add more sons unto him. He was also given a promise from God, so he knew God could restore his son. (Read the chapter for full context and understanding if you don't know the story.)

We do not know how God will try us, but we all have to go through our seasons of testing. God knows each of us and what we are capable of; that is what He intends to bring out of us. He Himself had placed that potential in us, so He knows us. Some of which can only be birthed after enduring through the fire and storms of life. Don't you want to be the best version of yourself?

Coping with Her Depression

Coping with her depression was not easy. It took me a long time to finally get it right. It began with the onset of puberty, her becoming withdrawn and wanting her own space. I was too busy to recognize the emotional support that she lacked, that I had stopped giving. We didn't talk much; we didn't play together anymore. What type of a relationship was that? Even with getting older, she loved us playing. I can imagine how neglected she felt, like her mother didn't love her anymore. I did; I was just too caught up in trying to fix things when I should be practicing what the Word said, to *rest* and let God. "Come unto me, all ye that labor and are heavy laden, and I will give you rest" (Matthew 11:28).

There was also another disorder I found out about through observation. Over time, I began to notice that every time her period was about to come, her whole mood and behavior changed. After doing some digging to understand it, I found that she might have premenstrual dysphoric disorder (PMDD). PMDD is a severe form of premenstrual syndrome. The symptoms are so severe that it affects the way the person who has it and their daily living tasks. I believe that when some of our girls display behaviors that were never there before, this can be a cause.

She began to act out by refusing to attend class, cursing, threatening to run away, of which she tried a few times, a few squabbles at school, and also exhibited signs of OCD. How did I, as a parent, manage all of that? I tried doing what the Word said, and it just felt like nothing was changing; it kept getting worse. Long nights at the hospital because she wanted to commit suicide, and all the prayers were just not working, or so I thought. She was diagnosed with major depression after the third evaluation. A simple definition of "depression" is when a person becomes hopeless, has no desire to live or see the future, has low self-esteem, sometimes feels suicidal and will attempt to harm themselves, does not care about anyone or themselves, does not care to practice self-hygiene and so on. Now, this definition is based on what I've seen, but anyone can google what depression is and what the signs and symptoms are.

After a few visits to the ER that led to admittance to the child's psych ER and twice on the ward, I gave up. I was now becoming withdrawn and tired; the sleepless nights, the fuss, the torment (as that is what it was). I was both mentally and physically drained. This was exactly where the devil wanted me.

I took a leave of absence from work as I had a lot of call-outs. I was less frequent in church, and I became a dry Christian. No serious prayer life, no Word life, only a few worships here and there. I was now becoming depressed myself. I saw a psychologist for an evaluation and began seeing a therapist. I only had a few sessions as finding time for myself was hard also. Realizing that I, too, was becoming affected, I got back into really seeking God. My thoughts were, if I am down and she is down, who will pick us up? I cannot fail her. There was a time when I also wanted to take some time off from college, and she encouraged me to continue. Now how is it that she was able to encourage me but couldn't do it for herself? I believe that was a way that God was letting me know that He was still there with me, even when I didn't acknowledge Him.

Can you imagine turning your back on the one thing that was constant in your life? The one thing that kept you? The one thing that is able to keep you from falling? Yes. Instead of submitting myself to the will of God, I fought against it, and it became so hard. No one can go against His will and still stand; He will surely fall. Look at the example of Saul, who became Paul; he had to succumb to God's will after being knocked off his horse and was blinded. He had to confess Christ as Lord. "We all fell down, and I heard a voice saying to me in Aramaic, 'Saul, Saul, why are you persecuting me? It is useless for you to fight against my will'" (Acts 26:14, NLT). Some of us need that same knocking as Saul got to really know ourselves and to know Christ. God knows how to reach each of us. God's will, will be accomplished, always. So go through the fire and allow God to do His work in you; it is useless to run as Jonah did, and it is useless to fight; you'll never win. I know that now. What was His will? To commune with Him, to seek in times of trouble, to cry out to Him and to do it consistently, to give Him thanks in all circumstances because that is His will for me. Not to give up but to press. "Be thankful in all circumstances, for this is God's will for you who belong to Christ Jesus" (1 Thessalonians 5:18, NLT). Though hard it may be, we cannot fail to give God thanks; it could be worse, nor do we know the full plan of God. We only know in part.

What I didn't know then was that God wanted me to change certain things about myself to be able to deal with the situation effectively. For instance, He gave me a word concerning my attitude and that I needed the spirit of gentleness. I was a little too harsh. What my pastor and friend, Pastor Smith, told me years later was that "God needed to sand away the rough contour. I was like sandpaper, and He needed me to be like the smoother side of a buffer." This was funny to me because He was so right. God cannot use us in our natural state as we are when we come to Him. He has to buff down and tone down the grit, still leaving a little, but tone enough to be graceful.

I was not ready for what God was and wanted to do in my life. God had to get me ready. God has called all of us out of darkness into His glorious light. When we come to the light, there are things still within us that He has to tone down or up. There are things that need to be put in place for Him to use us as He intended when He created us. Paul said it rightly in his letter to Timothy when he described the different vessels in a great house.

> *But in a great house there are not only vessels of gold and of silver, but also of wood and of earth; and some to honor, and some to dishonor. If a man therefore purge himself from these, he shall be a vessel unto honor, sanctified, and meet for the master's use, and prepared unto every good work.*
>
> — 2 Timothy 2:20–21

I also love the NLT's version as it offers a clearer insight into being pure for God's use.

*In a wealthy home some utensils are made of gold
and silver, and some are made of wood and clay. The
expensive utensils are used for special occasions, and
the cheap ones are for everyday use. If you keep yourself
pure, you will be a special utensil for honorable use.
Your life will be clean, and you will be ready for the
Master to use you for every good work.*

— 2 Timothy 2:20–21 (NLT)

I needed the refiner's fire to be made pure. A vessel fit and sanctified for God's use. God wants to make all of us vessels of honor, but it starts with Jesus. Recognizing that we need Him, we need saving. We are filthy and messed up without Him. I don't care how good you might feel about yourself. We are nothing at all without Christ. I am nothing without God. What God did for me, He wants to do the same for you, but are you willing to endure hardship as a good soldier? Are we willing to pay the cost and make the sacrifice?

So, I was too hard on my child and myself. When I needed to show mercy or grace, I yelled at her, and if I could, maybe I would've slapped her too. I didn't understand the mental pain that she was experiencing, and she needed me to be softer and kinder, but I wasn't. Maybe if I was more understanding, then I would have been kinder to her, and the many fights and bad behaviors could have been avoided resulting in much more peace of mind.

I came from a place where people do not believe in mental illness, especially in children. We say, "What do children have to worry about? They don't have to work or have bills to pay."

While the latter is true, they do experience different emotions that, if not channeled correctly, can affect them. Depression does not just appear out of the blue. It takes time to build up and can be triggered by certain events. Now I am not a psychiatrist or specialist in the field of mental illness, but I can tell you from what I've seen and experienced. What I also know is that all mental illnesses are not a part of God's plan. Trauma or some other traumatic experience can trigger such illnesses, as well as it can be hereditary (transferred by spirits/evil altars in the family), but it all takes place in the spiritual realm before manifesting in the physical. Now here is where the enemy comes in and plays on the minds of the unknowing victim, and the traumatic experience now leads to mental illness.

Here is what the Word says in Isaiah 53:5, "But he was wounded for our transgressions, he was bruised for our iniquities: the chastisement of our peace was upon him; and with his stripes we are healed." As children of God, we are healed because of Christ's finished works on the cross. Therefore, we should not be afflicted with illness. If and when it comes, we are to declare what God had said in His Word. He does honor His Word above His name. We are not to agree with the enemy when he comes to us; run from him. Your child is lying, do not call the child a liar, pray and declare that they are truthful. Begin to thank God that your child is delivered and ask God to destroy the gateway that the enemy uses to enter. Destroy by fire every evil altar set up against our children, in Jesus' name. If that altar is not destroyed, it will continue to work against you. You will not prosper until it is destroyed. The Word of God says, "My people perish because of a lack of knowledge."

I used to hear people say, "What you don't know can't hurt you." What a *big* lie from the enemy. What I didn't know certainly hurt me and not only me but those around me. What a deception. We have been deceived into thinking and believing superstition and fables created centuries ago by the enemy and passed down from generation to generation by our forefathers. We must awake from our slumber and serve that old serpent notice. Stop living a lie.

If we repeat a thing a lot, it suddenly starts to sound true, and that is what the enemy wants. Now imagine a person who wholeheartedly believes such a statement. There is no convincing such as one that the statement is wrong. The stronghold has been set up in his mind, and it will only take the truth, the Word of God, to break such beliefs. Now, we wonder why we go through the pressing and the fiery trials. Our mindsets must be changed. Our behavior needs correcting. God didn't cause the problem, but He'll allow it to bring a good change in the life of a believer and to get the glory whilst putting the enemy to shame. So, when we fail, there is no rejoicing in it. God is not glorified, and the devil laughs. I cannot afford to let the enemy laugh at my expense; no, not anymore. It is hard to do what you know that you are to do when in a situation, but it takes persistence and consistency to really see results.

I remember coming home from class, and the apartment was a mess. Sheets on the floor, dressers naked with body lotion and body oil poured out on the floor. It was like an earthquake took place while I was away. All she did was smile at me. What would you do in such a situation as mine? Beat, slap, punish, yell, etc. What I did was take something she loved and get rid of it. That didn't do anything. I gave her a good scolding, but all she did was mimic me. One would say that she was demonized, and yes, there was a spirit involved, but I believe that the enemy used her to get to me. You see, the enemy knows our weakness; he knows which buttons to press; remember, the goal is to get me to curse God, give up on God, on life, that my purpose would not be realized. The enemy taunted me for days. Prayer and fasting didn't help, plus I had also given up during some seasons of the whole ordeal. I also was not praying accurately. I prayed but often failed to declare what I desired to see instead of what I was seeing. Replace the negative with the Word of God concerning our lives and the plan God has for us. If my child is sick, her purpose is not being realized. Her years are being wasted, but I thank God for His mercy. He will not leave us forever. If we continue to seek and push, He will make a way. All we need is faith that God can and the staying power to remain in prayer. God will reveal things to us, but we must be paying attention. Look for the answers to the things that we're praying about.

For me, I was praying about too many things at once, as God does answers, but I miss it because I'm putting in so many requests. Thus, I fail to recognize what exactly God is answering to. I did not focus on the main issues at hand and awaited God's answer. Let's say I have a pressing issue at hand. Before going to bed, I make it my only focus as I want to know and understand clearly when the answer comes. Now, this does not mean that I don't pray otherwise, but more emphasis is placed on the issue at hand. How I coped with her depression was God at work in me, bringing the change in her.

What I found out only came through spending time in His presence consistently. This was where God began to open my understanding. He led me to some teachings, to the fellowship I'm presently a part of. My life changed totally when I began to see God in a new light. The day I changed my mind and began to see and behave how my Father said that I should, everything that I once knew shattered, and I was never the same.

Deliverance Came Slowly

As I began to change my attitude, my mindset, and my ways, I began to see the changes in our relationship, the changes in her. As I allowed God to work on me, He was also doing something in her. I gave myself to the change, though it wasn't easy but being practical led to a habit that encouraged the change. As God showed me what I was doing wrong, He taught me how to handle each situation that arose. The more I gave myself to being obedient and being practical, the more God showed me and the more He fixed.

You see, the work had to begin in me before it could reach her. I was the problem. I refused to let God have His way, and when I decided to give myself away, that was the beginning of a slow and sure journey to victory. One by one, things were unraveling, the darkness became light, and I knew exactly how to pray for victory.

Now I'm not saying that I caused what happened, nor did anyone, but my response to the situation. What was I doing wrong; what did I fail to see? I did so many things wrong: giving up, failing in consistent prayer, and not recognizing the evil altars. I recognized some of the spirits at work but forgot the altars. My lack of knowledge, lack of wisdom, and lack of understanding slowed the change process. But when the light came, and knowledge increased, darkness must flee.

I remember one night, in a dream, I was digging out a foundation and throwing the rubbles away. This was God showing me that the problem was lying in the foundation, and I was destroying the evil foundation. This revelation came from the mercies and goodness of God. It came through consistent prayer. I woke up and prayed, asking God to continue to destroy every foundation that He did not lay and to send His fire to destroy it and leave no remnant of it.

God, in His mercy, came to my aid. Many times the Lord spoke to me in dreams, and as I continued to press in Him, things became clearer along with the help and wisdom of my friend and pastor. I cannot begin to describe all that was happening in the trial but trust me, it was like hell on earth. At least, that was how I felt. To see God the Father show up how He did amazed me. I am forever thankful.

I was led down a path where I had to examine every angle of the situation. Where, what, when, how. When that was done, and the problem still lingered, here was when the work on my mindset began. I later understood that our faulty mindsets are strongholds that the enemy fortifies. The things we grew up believing and applying them to our Christian lives can be very dangerous. This is why seeking God, seeking knowledge, seeking wisdom, getting understanding, and prayer are of utmost importance. Seek council from a wise person if and when necessary. How will you know that they are wise? Check their story. Does it match their lifestyle? Does it align with God? Does what they say come to pass or help in difficult or not so difficult situations? Also, pray about it. Prayer should be the first option when seeking wisdom from an individual. Ask God who to speak to for council. He'll tell you, show you, or even lead the person to you. That person that comes to mind, ask them. If you have to question it, pray some more and wait.

We will not understand every situation, and after doing all that we are told to do by God and still no change, we have to keep standing, keep trusting, and keep praying. In the Book of Daniel, when he prayed concerning a matter, the answer to his question was answered by God, but Daniel didn't know this at the time. He had no idea that God had sent the answer the moment he began praying. Daniel prayed for twenty-one days before receiving the answer that was sent the very first day he prayed. What if Daniel had given up the nineteenth or twentieth day? When we look at it now, we would call it madness and probably say he could've waited another day. I'm saying to you, wait another day and keep on waiting. It's always easy to judge a situation when we're not the ones in it. But all judgment belongs to God. He knows everything that we don't and can see everything that we can't (Daniel 10). We also must remember that we wrestle not against flesh and blood but against principalities and powers. Therefore, we must press in prayer and practical living of the Word of God. No practice, no perfection, no word knowledge, no firepower/sword to wield, no bullets to fire, and definitely, no Dunamis.

> *For we wrestle not against flesh and blood, but against principalities, against powers, against the rulers of the darkness of this world, against spiritual wickedness in high places. Wherefore take unto you the*

whole armour of God, that ye may be able to with-
stand in the evil day, and having done all, to stand.

— Ephesians 6:12–13

As mentioned in chapter 6, we also have to be clothed in the full armor of God to be able to withstand the evil. Can a soldier go to war without his protective uniform? This includes his helmet or cap, his combat boot, his combat uniform (ACU), his belt, and his gun. Likewise, we cannot face the enemy naked. Be filled with the Spirit of God dressed in full armor. As you read further in Ephesians 6, you'll see exactly what these armors are and what they represent.

Imagine facing your enemy naked; what does that mean for the naked soldier? I wouldn't want to know, because I've seen too many movies in the past. If someone hates you with cruel hatred, don't expect them to play with you unawares. They will kill. "Consider mine enemies; for they are many; and they hate me with cruel hatred" (Psalm 25:19). Can you understand when someone hates you? Now imagine them hating you with cruel hatred. This is how much the enemies hate us. And we best believe that anything or anyone that opposes God is an enemy; likewise, we are considered enemies to the devil because we trust in God.

Attend unto me, and hear me: I mourn in my com-
plaint, and make a noise; because of the voice of the
enemy, because of the oppression of the wicked: for they
cast iniquity upon me, and in wrath they hate me.

— Psalm 55:2–3

The Psalmist had to cry for help because of the voice of his enemy that oppressed him. He invited God to intervene in the situation.

As the chapter states, deliverance came slowly; it did. For us, it wasn't all at once. Some deliverance happens over time, while others can be instantaneous, depending on the situation. Deliverance is also progressive. The more light is shed on an area of darkness, victory beams, and God is glorified. For example, I was praying about a situation without all the facts, and my prayer was missing the intended target. In a war, you have to be as accurate as possible. Hence sometimes, a sharpshooter is needed to remove a target that is or can potentially cause major damage. Let's say, in my case, I need to hit the intended target, the big man that is the root of my problems. If I shoot at the ones around the intended target and keep missing the target itself, my problem will still remain. This big man, this target, should be my focus as he is the root cause of all my problems.

So, I was hitting the little ticky-tacky fishes and not the whale. How can I get released until this big whale is gone? This whale is always hiding. As big as he is, I wasn't hitting it. Then God, by His mercy, gave knowledge and wisdom to hit this whale. The knowledge and wisdom here is the light that has been shed on how to get the whale. Applying what is now light to the situation brings victory.

Knowledge and wisdom did not come overnight. Much prayer and seeking God opened the door for Him to respond. Where there is lack of understanding to the response from God, it can also delay the victory as one may not know how to pray after receiving the light. Sometimes there will also be hiccups or minor setbacks after a win, but the goal is to believe that you have won. So, whatever is showing its ugly head now, must go. For instance, I noticed some changes in Kiki's behavior; then, after a while, the same behavior came back. Here is what the Word says concerning this.

When an evil spirit leaves a person, it goes into the desert, searching for rest. But when it finds none, it says, 'I will return to the person I came from.' So it returns and finds that its former home is all swept and in order. Then the spirit finds seven other spirits more evil than itself, and they all enter the person and live there. And so that person is worse off than before.

— Luke 11:24–26 (NLT)

Now, she was not possessed but being oppressed by this evil spirit. I know that God had done a work in us. I believed God's Word concerning her. Was I supposed to think that the spirit was back? Nope, it was only trying to come in, and if I had agreed with it by distrusting God and speaking negatively, it would have surely taken up room in her and brought other wicked spirits as well.

If you believe in God that the prayer you prayed worked, God heard, that He delivered, that God honors His Word, do not look at the dust. This is where the enemy wants to come back, and if you revert to the old belief and way of speaking or doing things, he now has access again. This means that you didn't trust God, you lacked faith in the Word, and you didn't trust the deliverance. The enemy will always seek to come back. Be on your guard; stay in prayer.

Now while the deliverance came slowly to us, God was also changing our environment. We moved from where we were. We had a change of MD; this also brought much light. After a few visits and one stressful situation, this doctor, who is also a native of our country, was able to figure out exactly what was happening with my daughter. This was also assessed to ensure accuracy. Let me say that I was on board 100 percent with the new findings.

The conclusion was later drawn that my child had a mild case of ADHD. This was one of the contributors to the depression. How did we get here? Through prayer and divine connection. All it took was a switch of the psychiatrist. This doctor understood my child even more than I did after listening to them conversate. God also released more information concerning her late father and ADHD. Everything has a root cause; some things are just manipulated by the enemy to mask the true cause. This is why we can never stop praying. We see depression, anxiety, etc., but what is the root? The moment we begin to pray, the Lord begins to release His grace for understanding to put things into place. But a lot of times we miss it. Why? We are not at the place where God wants us. We are not in tune with the Holy Spirit. We lack the wisdom and knowledge to be practical. We know the Word, but we don't understand what to do.

Sometimes we see people upset for no reason but what got them there. One word can trigger a foolish quarrel. I used to work in customer service, and I saw a lot of angry people. It's like when people wake up angry, and they come to the store and let it all out on the cashier, supervisors, and even other customers who are trying to help them. There is always an underlying cause. No one gets upset for no reason. Something or someone caused it. This is where wisdom says, "This person is not mad at me; something deeper is going on." We cannot take it personal in this case.

In the case of the enemy fighting against us, we must and have to take it personal. Get radical and chant fire. Pretty prayers won't work. You cannot be in a ditch and say, "Help, help." You have to yell from the bottom of your lungs, "*Help, help!!! Jesus!!*" When the blind beggar at the roadside heard Jesus was coming, he didn't care that people were telling him to shut up! He yelled all the more for Jesus. The story is found in Luke 18:35–43 (NLT); I've highlighted verses 37–42,

> *They told him that Jesus the Nazarene was going by. So he began shouting, 'Jesus, Son of David, have mercy on me!' 'Be quiet!' the people in front yelled at him. But he only shouted louder, 'Son of David, have mercy on me!' When Jesus heard him, he stopped and ordered that the man be brought to him. As the man came near, Jesus asked him, 'What do you want me to do for you?' 'Lord,' he said, 'I want to see!' And Jesus said, 'All right, receive your sight! Your faith has healed you.'*
>
> — Luke 18:37–42 (NLT)

We need to cry out like blind Bartimaeus for Jesus and don't stop no matter what people are saying or how foolish you may feel. At one point, I felt like people must think something was wrong with me, why I was serving God and all these problems. This is where we have also messed up the body of Christ. The moment we came to Christ, our warfare just began. Many will preach that everything will be alright. Not so. Your soul will be saved, but problems will hit you; why? The enemy wants to come back. He wants to have you, and if your attitude, your behavior, your response is not right, you'll have no peace.

We must cry out to Jesus for help in difficult situations; remember, David also cried for help because of the oppression of the wicked. Imagine if this man had listened to the crowd, he would not have received his sight. Growing up, I've heard the saying, "Closed mouths don't get fed." If my mouth is closed, how will God know that I need Him? He gave me dominion over the earth, so if I don't invite Him into my situation, He will not intervene. Mankind has power on earth, according to Genesis 1:26. The devil tricked Adam and took that dominion we had, but when Christ came, the Bible says, "He made a shew of them openly, triumphing over them in it" (Colossians 2:15). Christ destroyed these powers and took back our dominion. He died on the cross for our sins to restore us to our Heavenly Father. He then gave us power to tread upon serpents. "Behold, I give unto you power to tread on serpents and scorpions, and over all the power of the enemy: and nothing shall by any means hurt you" (Luke 10:19). Many of us don't even trust the power that we have or even know it. Use what you have and start there; God will do the rest when He sees your faithfulness. Keep building, keep growing in the Spirit.

I must say that therapy is also good. There is a lot of information and help that is given and discussed in a session that can and will help the individuals (parents, children, etc.) to overcome or help the person to fight the negative thoughts. The tools given are to be put into practice. On the other hand, there is medication, and like I said, this did not work for us and will not work because these illnesses are rooted in spiritual darkness. Depression and its cousins are influenced by a spirit, and this spirit(s) is not of God. A thought in the mind that keeps on replaying until the enemy says, "Here we come now you can't break free." I believe medication only suppresses or hides what is really the main problem. At the end of the day, the problem is still there, tucked under a whole lot of to-dos. Go to therapy, take meds, do this, do that, but the big boss is still in hiding, and any moment can show its ugly head.

I declared,

> To appoint unto them that mourn in Zion, to give
> unto them beauty for ashes, the oil of joy for mourning,
> the garment of praise for the spirit of heaviness; that
> they might be called trees of righteousness, the plant-
> ing of the LORD, that he might be glorified.
>
> —Isaiah 61:3

The garment of praise was upon her. This took care of the spirit of heaviness. Depression is a spirit of heaviness; it weighs the victims down. The famous minister, Derek Prince, had depression and got delivered when he began to declare Joel 2, which says that "Whosoever shall call upon the name of the Lord, shall be saved." You may even feel like it's you doing or saying the bad things you do, but it is the spirit at work in you. This was also why I needed gentleness to deal with my daughter.

God did not call us to live a suppressed life. To be bogged down by demons. The enemy plays on our thoughts; all our battles are in the mind. There is a saying that goes, "From you can perceive it, you can achieve it." This is true. We think of negative thoughts so much that we start to believe them. I am not beautiful, I'll never be good enough, I'll never get into that college, I'll never get that job, that spouse, the house, etc., and we talk ourselves out of the blessing. Who said that you are not good enough? David knew his father, and he declared that he was fearfully and wonderfully made (Psalm 139:14). In Genesis chapter 1, when God created man, He saw that it was good. We were created good. The enemy will sow seeds unawares, and we now begin to believe the lies. Whose report will you believe today, the One who made you or the outcast Satan who is jealous of us and hates us? What did the Word of God say concerning us? This is what we must believe, "it is written." How will you know what is written? It begins with the Bible. Read it. It is the only authoritative word of God. Meditate upon these scriptures as nothing is merely from men, but the Holy Spirit which came from God to man.

Knowing this first, that no prophecy of the scripture is
of any private interpretation. For the prophecy came

not in old time by the will of man: but holy men of
God spake as they were moved by the Holy Ghost.

— 2 Peter 1:20–21

All scripture is given by inspiration of God, and is
profitable for doctrine, for reproof, for correction, for
instruction in righteousness: that the man of God may
be perfect, thoroughly furnished unto all good works.

— 2 Timothy 3:16–17

Throughout all that I have been through, which is too much to write here, God has never changed. This experience drew me closer to God and gave me life. I know that I only know in part, and the more I seek God, the more I know Him, the more I desire what He desires, the more I pray His will, and the more I die to myself. The more I prayed, the more the chains fell, and revelation came. At the same time, God was and still is doing work in me.

Today my daughter is almost finished with high school and looking at colleges. Her attendance and grades are back on track, and she is doing super well. Only the grace and favor of God could have done that. She listens more, is more helpful, and is an emerging editor (she loves to edit videos). Not everything is perfect; she's still a budding teenager, so I still have to be on top of things. There are behaviors that need to be changed, but that will change when she begins to seek God again. I pray the day that she draws near to God as she once did and lives according to His Word. I do believe that God will also use her to bless others like herself. There is nothing that God cannot and will not do for those who come to Him.

As for myself, it is so funny how the Lord placed me in a job that I did not apply for. I, however, took the position as it was flexible and a good fit at the time. So, I now work with the developmentally disabled and, in some cases, those with mental disorders. I call it a setup. But I was in training with my daughter. I am still pressing and still learning. We can never get tired of learning, never get tired of praying, never get tired of fighting. Victory does not mean the fight is over totally. We continue to pray as the Word said; the devil goes about like a roaring lion, seeking whom he may devour. We must stay on guard and be on the offense.

Upon finishing this book, I had a dream where I saw my child in a cage, and then she was free. But before she got freed, I saw a dark cloud lifted from her chest area. I believe this to be an evil spirit. The spirit that was tormenting her. She is free. Remember when I started, I said she was not totally free, and I asked, "Lord, how can I write when there are still things that need to be corrected in my child." I could see the changes, but it was upon finishing the book I saw the spirit leaving. I came into agreement with what God has done in the spirit to see the physical manifestation. What a God! Thank You, Jesus, all glory to our God.

Conclusion

As I come to a close, some may not agree with what I'm saying. That's okay. I know that more than some will agree with me. I have released what the Holy Spirit has led me to release, so I know that there are people who are and have gone through what I have. These are the people I want to speak to. Mothers, single parents, fathers, relatives, you are not alone.

I want to encourage you today, no matter what your situation is. It may not be a mental illness, but whatever it is, God can. His word said that Jesus came not for the whole but to those that are sick. What is your sickness today? Jesus, the Healer, desires to work on your behalf. Will you trust Him today? I did not know what to do in the midst of the situation when the battle became tremendously hot. I tried medication, but it did not work. The doctors will say it takes six to twelve months before we can see any improvement. I must say that she never took the meds that long, but we could see that this was more than what the doctors knew. I did some research and found some supplements that could help. I spoke to the psychiatrist about it, and she advised me well. Some will not tell you because it goes against their creed; they can only advise on generic drugs. Do your own research based on the signs and symptoms your child has and go from there, don't sit back and accept everything the doctors say. Though the doctors have vast knowledge and will advise based on such, many do not know that certain things are spiritually discerned. Who knows more than God? No one. After Kiki began taking the supplement, I found her mood began to improve when it came to that time of the month because of the PMDD.

When the enemy tormented me for days, and I had no release, I gave up as the pressure became overbearing, don't let that be you. God wants to help us, but, as I said before, if we don't invite Him into the situation, how can He help? What I said might seem strange to the unbelieving. But I know what I've been through. I know what I've seen. I know how God showed up. I did not note every single thing that happened; some things are too hurtful to write. If it had not been for Jesus, I'd be dead already.

Some things I've seen in the realm of the spirit cannot be shared here. I've shared a little to show that I know what I am saying. If we are not seeking God about our situation, how will we know why it's there, from whence it came, and how to deal with it. It's funny how people will go to mediums/witches and the like to get help, not knowing that these people work with the same evil spirit that they're up against. The problem will only mask itself but is still there. This also opens the door for other negative things to happen to the person and their family. These negative things can be poverty, being always in a bad relationship, no stability, children being out of control, etc. We invite trouble when we step out of God's will. This is why we pray and repent because of the sins of our fore-parents. Have you noticed a negative pattern in your family that can be an altar that was raised by the enemy because of what your ancestors did? How do I know such things? Experience, the Word of God, and revelation.

Why not seek the Creator who gave life. Can I ask a cup to operate as a pot? No, we must seek the Creator regarding our life. God, why am I here? God, help me to function in the area You created me to. It begins with repentance. Change your mindset; change what culture and tradition have taught you. We must follow IT IS WRITTEN. Written where? Written in God's Word. Follow the Holy Spirit, your guide. Trust God to do the impossible even when things seem hard and grim. Live a life that pleases God. Be kind to one another, don't envy, don't boast, don't murmur, don't complain. Develop the mind to suffer, give thanks in all things, and don't forget to pray, pray, pray.

Be Encouraged

L et your trials push you closer to God, and yes, don't forget to praise and give thanks in the midst of it all. I found out that this is a sure way to be free of pain, stress and to find peace. It also glorifies God and confuses the enemy. Raise a hallelujah and shame the enemy. Trust me; it's not easy; it certainly won't be but take baby steps until you find that rhythm. Have the mind of Christ. He had the mind to suffer; after all, that was His main purpose, to suffer for you and for me. If we have the mind to suffer, nothing can move us if suffering comes.

> *Forasmuch then as Christ hath suffered for us in the flesh, arm yourselves likewise with the same mind: for he that hath suffered in the flesh hath ceased from sin; that he no longer should live the rest of his time in the flesh to the lusts of men, but to the will of God.*

> — 1 Peter 4:1–2

Another thing, we cannot face our battles without the help of the Holy Spirit. We are not complete without God. If we suffer as Christians, imagine those who are without Christ. Our suffering is not unto death because we know Christ. We have mortified the deeds of the flesh and live because He lives. The man without Christ is dead. A dead man cannot fight. The Holy Spirit reveals the deep things of God, and without Him, we can know nothing. If you are a friend of Christ, keep pushing; if you do not know Him, get to know Him. Jesus is the only answer to our problems, even though we will still have problems because we live in a fallen world. Do not let your circumstances speak for you. Let the Spirit of God do the speaking, working in you the will of God for your life. There will always be a battle to fight, whether we are saved or unsaved. The only difference is that the unsaved do not perceive that they are in a fight. They seek to blame others and not the real culprit. Most of those who are saved know what they are up against, but there is good news for you. There is peace in Jesus as He gives us His peace. If Christ is in our vessel, we can ride out any storm, and we will arrive at our destination safely. Do not worry; God has this, and He has you if you'll let Him in. Today, if you hear His voice, harden not your heart. If you are convicted, turn to Him. Reach out to those who have a genuine relationship with Christ and go from there, be it via YouTube, Facebook messages, email, etc. God has you, and most of all, He loves you.

Bibliography

Bible Exposition. "Longsuffering." https://bibleveryday.com/merciful-gracious-longsuffering Accessed November 27, 2021.

Books of the Bible. https://www.biblestudytools.com/books-of-the-bible/

Dr. Munroe, Myles. *Discover the Hidden You: The secret to living the good life.* (Shippensburg: Destiny Image Publishers, Inc., 2021).

Premenstrual Dysphoric Disorder (PMDD). https://www.hopkinsmedicine.org/health/conditions-and-diseases/premenstrual-dysphoric-disorder-pmdd#:~:text=Premenstrual%20dysphoric%20disorder%20(PMDD)%20is,medicines%20can%20help%20manage%20symptoms

The Bible. Authorized King James Version, Oxford UP, 1998. https://www.kingjamesbibleonline.org

The Chosen. TV Series.

About the Author

Melissa Samuels is a mother and a lover of God. She is a woman of God that is highly devoted to her calling. She firmly believes and is also convinced that the kingdom of God should be the first priority in one's life. She believes that kingdom advancement should be the primary goal of every person on this planet. As a result of such conviction, she is loyal in her devotion to God with her time, energy, and resources in word, deed, and truth.

Melissa is committed to the assignment placed upon her life by God. She is a great lover of children and one that commits herself by going above and beyond in whatever way necessary to seek the welfare of a child's spiritual uplifting and spiritual empowerment so that they can become an asset to this crooked and perverse generation.

Melissa is a servant of God that believes that someone should always be there to pass on the mantle to. With such conviction and passion, she considers it an urgent cry for this generation to be aligned with God to be able to receive. She believes that nurturing a child spiritually from an early age is very important to the cultivation of their spiritual life; so as to develop a kingdom culture at a young age.

CPSIA information can be obtained
at www.ICGtesting.com
Printed in the USA
LVHW011205190522
719134LV00012B/286